I Will Build My Church

Frank Duprée

ISBN: 1537771329
ISBN-13: 9781537771328

DEDICATION

I want to dedicate this book to my parents, Frank and Phyllis Duprée. They took the words of Jesus literally and left everything they had to plant Living Water Church, Riverhead, NY.

My Father was a successful businessman owning his own Advertising company and my Mother was also an Entrepreneur who created her own cosmetic company and also trained young women to be models and raised 6 children. They sold it all and gave it to The Lord!

They became Pillars in the Church and served the Body of Christ as an Apostle and a Prophetess/Teacher. No one ever had better parents than I did. I am grateful that at the time of this writing in 2016 they are still alive and still serving The Lord in His Church.

Frank Duprée

ACKNOWLEDGMENTS

I want to acknowledge Dr. Frank Damazio who planted the seed of this book inside of me many years ago when he spoke at a Ministers Conference in NYC. He brought up the concept of "reeds, stones and pillars" in a message and the phrase stuck with me. It was that "seed" that grew into this book.

CONTENTS

Chapter 1

TRANSFORMATION

Matthew 16:18   Jesus said: "…I will build my Church"

The Church is a "Spiritual Building" and is therefore not built with material things. Jesus has been building the Church with people since the day of Pentecost and He will continue to build it with people until He comes again. In this book I want to show you the Transformation that Jesus desires to see in all of us by looking at three different types of people found in the church: **REEDS, STONES & PILLARS**.

Everyone starts out as a Reed Person and if they allow the Holy Spirit to work in their life they will begin the Transformation into a Stone Person. Only those who truly allow the process of Transfiguration in their life can become Pillars in the Church.

Of these three types of people, The Lord can use two of these in the building of the Church. They are the **STONES** and the **PILLARS**. God does not use the **REEDS** as He builds the Church because they are unstable. It's not that Reed People are not saved it's just that they just stay saved and never become Disciples. The reed nature in all of us must be transformed or we cannot really become of part of the House of God.

Let's look at some Old Testament Scriptures to see the shadows that the New Testament presents as reality. In each of these we will need to discuss the key parts of the verses…

1 Kings 5:17, 18 At the king's command, they quarried large blocks of high-quality stone and shaped them to make the foundation of the Temple. Men from the city of Gebal helped Solomon's and Hiram's carpenters to hew and prepare the timber and **the stonesquarers shaped the stone** for the Temple.

1 Kings 6:7 " And while **the temple was built with stones that were finished at the quarry,** so that no hammer, or chisel or any iron tool was heard in the temple while it was being built".

I Peter 2:5 "…and you are **living stones being used by God to build up** his spiritual house"

2 Chronicles 3:15-17 "Also he made in the front of the house **two pillars** thirty and five cubits high each… one on the right hand, and the other on the left ; and called the name of that on the right hand **Jachin (He establishes),** and the name of that on the left **Boaz (In Him is strength).**

Rev. 3:12 "Whoever is an overcomer will I make into a **Pillar** in the temple of my God"

In the Old Testament we see

"types and shadows" of the Stones & Pillars

In the New Testament we see that

the stones and pillars are people!

Jesus said He would build His Church. He is building it with people whom He calls "**living stones**" and "**pillars**".

In building the Temple Solomon did not have as difficult a job as the Lord does in building His Church because it is much easier to shape a stone and a pillar than it is to change a person's nature.

In the building of the Church **The Holy Spirit works through the Set Man as a "Master Builder"** and **the Elders as the cutters and stonesquarers**.

And, the Glory of the latter house, the Church, will far exceed the glory of the former house, Solomon's temple!

Since we all start off as "Reeds" when we are saved we need to identify and understand it so we can eliminate it from our lives.

Chapter 2

THE REED NATURE

In **John 1:35-42** Jesus confronts Peter and says to him; "You are **Simon (a reed),** you shall be called **Peter (a stone).** Simon has to go through a *CHANGE OF NATURE* in order to fulfill God's will.

A reed may be beautiful to look at but it is w*eak, fragile and untrustworthy.* All you need to do is to squeeze a reed a little bit and it will bruise. So, moving from the "shadow" of the reed to the reality of "Reed People" we can see that they are

a. Weak = Easily Offended

b. Fragile = Quickly Discouraged

c. Untrustworthy = Easily swayed by circumstances or emotions

Even though they may look good on the outside and they may have charisma and a desire to do great things, their desire is not changed into action. What they actually do is develop the **"Outer Man"** and not the **"Inner Man".**

The 7 Characteristics of the "Reed Nature"

1.   **Matthew 14:22-31 (ESV)** Immediately he made the disciples get into the boat and go before him to the other side, while he dismissed the crowds. And after he had dismissed the crowds, he went up on the mountain by himself to pray. When evening came, he was there alone, but the boat by this time was a long way from the land, beaten by the waves, for the wind was against them. And in the fourth watch of the night he came to them, walking on the sea.

    But when the disciples saw him walking on the sea, they were terrified, and said, "It is a ghost!" and they cried out in fear. But immediately Jesus spoke to them, saying, "Take heart; it is I. Do not be afraid."

    And Peter answered him, "Lord, if it is you, command me to come to you on the water." He said, "Come." So Peter got out of the boat and walked on the water and came to Jesus.

    But when he saw the wind, he was afraid, and beginning to sink he cried out, "Lord, save me."

    Jesus immediately reached out his hand and took hold of him, saying to him, "O you of little faith, why did you doubt?"

    a. Reed people respond to circumstances and not to God

b. They may not care what others think but when things go wrong they don't realize how much of a mess they have made until they are way over their head and have to cry out for help.

c. They react much too quickly acting on their impulses rather than being led by the Holy Spirit and responding to God through prayer and meditation.

In this section of Scripture we see that Reed People are impulsive, hasty and impatient.

2.   **Matthew 15:10-16**

And he called the people to him and said to them, "Hear and understand: "It is not what goes into the mouth that defiles a person, but what comes out of the mouth; this defiles a person."

Then the disciples came and said to him, "Do you know that the Pharisees were offended when they heard this saying?"

He answered, "Every plant that my heavenly Father has not planted will be rooted up. Let them alone; they are blind guides. And if the blind lead the blind, both will fall into a pit."

But Peter said to him, "Explain the parable to us."

And he said, "Are you also still without understanding?

Here we see that Reed People are slow to understand the significance of spiritual things. Peter was looking for something "deep" and couldn't see that what Jesus was talking about was not a parable but a clear teaching.

3.   **Matthew 16:16-21 (ESV)**

Simon Peter replied, "You are the Christ, the Son of the living God."
And Jesus answered him, "Blessed are you, Simon Bar-Jonah! For flesh and blood has not revealed this to you, but my Father who is in heaven. And I tell you, you are Peter, and on this rock I will build my church, and the gates of hell shall not prevail against it. I will give you the keys of the kingdom of heaven, and whatever you bind on earth shall be bound in heaven, and whatever you loose on earth shall be loosed in heaven."

Then he strictly charged the disciples to tell no one that he was the Christ. From that time Jesus began to show his disciples that he must go to Jerusalem and suffer many things from the elders and chief priests and scribes, and be killed, and on the third day be raised.

Reed People are "blown with the wind". They are Spiritual one minute and Carnal the next.

a. Peter receives revelation that Jesus is the Christ

b. Jesus teaches about the cross.

c. Peter takes a hold of him by the shoulders and rebukes him.

4. **Matthew 17:1-5 (ESV)**

And after six days Jesus took with him Peter and James, and John his brother, and led them up a high mountain by themselves. And he was transfigured before them, and his face shone like the sun, and his clothes became white as light. And behold, there appeared to them Moses and Elijah, talking with him.

And Peter said to Jesus, "Lord, it is good that we are here. If you wish, I will make three tents here, one for you and one for Moses and one for Elijah."

He was still speaking when, behold, a bright cloud overshadowed them, and a voice from the cloud said, "This is my beloved Son, with whom I am well pleased; listen to him."

Reed People may try to appear spiritual but they are not.

a. Peter says, "Hey, it's good that we're here…"

b. God the Father interrupts him and tells him: "Hey, this is my Son, let Him do the talking!"

5. **Matthew 17:24-27 (ESV)**

When they came to Capernaum, the collectors of the two-drachma tax went up to Peter and said, "Does your teacher not pay the tax?"

He said, "Yes." And when he came into the house, Jesus spoke to him first, saying, "What do you think, Simon? From whom do kings of the earth take toll or tax? From their sons or from others?"

And when he said, "From others," Jesus said to him, "Then the sons are free.

However, not to give offense to them, go to the sea and cast a hook and take the first fish that comes up, and when you open its mouth you will find a shekel. Take that and give it to them for me and for yourself."

This is a significant aspect and we all need to see this desire that resides deep with all of us; The "reed person" wants to be important.

a. Peter speaks for Jesus and Jesus stops him at the door on his way into the house. "Hey Simon, what was that you were telling that guy about me?"

b. Jesus has to do a miracle to fix up Peter's mistakes. I wonder if Peter had enough sense to bring the fish home for dinner!

6. **Matthew 26:36-40 (ESV)**

Then Jesus went with them to a place called Gethsemane, and he said to his disciples, "Sit here, while I go over there and pray."

And taking with him Peter and the two sons of Zebedee, he began to be sorrowful and troubled. Then he said to them, "My soul is very sorrowful, even to death; remain here, and watch with me." And going a little farther he fell on his face and prayed, saying, "My Father, if it be possible, let this cup pass from me; nevertheless, not as I will, but as you will."

And he came to the disciples and found them sleeping. And he said to Peter, "So, could you not watch with me one hour?

From this Scripture it is clear to see that Reed People do not understand the significance of key situations.

    a.   Thinks Gethsemane is "just another prayer meeting"

    b.   Misses God's Best!

7.   **John 18:10,11 (ESV)**

Then Simon Peter, having a sword, drew it and struck the high priest's servant and cut off his right ear. (The servant's name was Malchus.) So Jesus said to Peter, "Put your sword into its sheath; shall I not drink the cup that the Father has given me?"

Reed People respond emotionally to pressure

    a.   Peter grabs his sword and cuts off the High Priest's servants ear.

    b.   Then he runs away.

We therefore have to conclude then that

a "reed person" is a "spiritual washout"!

Here is a perfect example of a Reed Person…

Mark 14:66-72 (ESV)

And as Peter was below in the courtyard, one of the servant girls of the high priest came, and seeing Peter warming himself, she looked at him and said, "You also were with the Nazarene, Jesus."

But he denied it, saying, "I neither know nor understand what you mean." And he went out into the gateway and the rooster crowed.

And the servant girl saw him and began again to say to the bystanders, "This man is one of them."

But again he denied it. And after a little while the bystanders again said to Peter, "Certainly you are one of them, for you are a Galilean."

But he began to invoke a curse on himself and to swear, "I do not know this man of whom you speak."

And immediately the rooster crowed a second time. And Peter remembered how Jesus had said to him, "Before the rooster crows twice, you will deny me three times." And he broke down and wept.

The Reed Person in all of us is a failure.

Simon Peter, still a "reed person" denies Jesus

    a. He goes by the fire and denies he knows Jesus 3 times. The third time he swears and denies him.

    b.   Jesus looks at him and he remembers the word, he goes away weeping.

There is nothing good in Simon Peter. He is a carnal person who doesn't get anything done for God. We all need to come to Jesus and admit that we have a "Reed Nature". We should repent of it and with a deep inner cry, ask Jesus to forgive us. We need to ask God to help us change. To take out the "Reed Nature" so we can be useful in the building up of that spiritual house, the Church.

How can we effect a change within our lives to "put off the old" and "put on the new"? We need to be "renewed in the 'spirit' or 'attitude' of our minds! **Ephesians 4:22-24**

When confronted with life's circumstances which will it be for you...

Reaction or Creation?

These two words contain the same letters...

It's your choice. Reed people will have a "reaction" rather than take the circumstances and make a "creation" out of it. When God saw that the world was without form and void He made a "creation". He did not just have a "reaction".

Use your mind to effect the change in your life. Focus your mind on what is necessary. Don't allow distractions to create havoc. Be in control.

Changing the reed nature is difficult but not half as bad as not changing will be!

In fact there are two roads you can take in life.

One says; "Life is difficult. It's full of trouble."

The other says; "Life is beautiful. It's full and rewarding."

Which road are you walking on?

Chapter 3

PREPARATION

To begin the next section we have to read from the Bible to get the background. So, here is the text from 1 Kings chapters 5 & 6

1 Kings 5 (ESV)

Now Hiram king of Tyre sent his servants to Solomon when he heard that they had anointed him king in place of his father, for Hiram always loved David. And Solomon sent word to Hiram, "You know that David my father could not build a house for the name of the LORD his God because of the warfare with which his enemies surrounded him, until the LORD put them under the soles of his feet. But now the LORD my God has given me rest on every side. There is neither adversary nor misfortune. And so I intend to build a house for the name of the LORD my God, as the LORD said to David my father, 'Your son, whom I will set on your throne in your place, shall build the house for my name.' Now therefore command that cedars of Lebanon be cut for me. And my servants will join your servants, and I will pay you for your servants such wages as you set, for you know that there is no one among us who knows how to cut timber like the Sidonians."

As soon as Hiram heard the words of Solomon, he rejoiced greatly and said, "Blessed be the LORD this day, who has given to David a wise son to be over this great people."

And Hiram sent to Solomon, saying, "I have heard the message that you have sent to me. I am ready to do all you desire in the matter of cedar and cypress timber. My servants shall bring it down to the sea from Lebanon, and I will make it into rafts to go by sea to the place you direct. And I will have them broken up there, and you shall receive it. And you shall meet my wishes by providing food for my household."

So Hiram supplied Solomon with all the timber of cedar and cypress that he desired, while Solomon gave Hiram 20,000 cors of wheat as food for his household, and 20,000 cors of beaten oil. Solomon gave this to Hiram year by year.

And the LORD gave Solomon wisdom, as he promised him. And there was peace between Hiram and Solomon, and the two of them made a treaty. King Solomon drafted forced labor out of all Israel, and the draft numbered 30,000 men. And he sent them to Lebanon, 10,000 a month in shifts. They would be a month in Lebanon and two months at home. Adoniram was in charge of the draft. Solomon also had 70,000 burden-bearers and 80,000 stonecutters in the hill country, besides Solomon's 3,300 chief officers who were over the work, who had charge of the people who carried on the work.

At the king's command they quarried out great, costly stones in order to lay the foundation of the house with dressed stones. So Solomon's builders and Hiram's builders and the men of Gebal did the cutting and prepared the timber and the stone to build the house.

1 Kings 6 (ESV)
In the four hundred and eightieth year after the people of Israel came out of the land of Egypt, in the fourth year of Solomon's reign over Israel, in the month of Ziv, which is the second month, he began to build the house of the LORD.

The house that King Solomon built for the LORD was sixty cubits long, twenty cubits wide, and thirty cubits high. The vestibule in front of the nave of the house was twenty cubits long, equal to the width of the house, and ten cubits deep in front of the house. And he made for the house windows with recessed frames. He also built a structure against the wall of the house, running around the walls of the house, both the nave and the inner sanctuary. And he made side chambers all around.

The lowest story was five cubits broad, the middle one was six cubits broad, and the third was seven cubits broad. For around the outside of the house he made offsets on the wall in order that the supporting beams should not be inserted into the walls of the house.

When the house was built, it was with stone prepared at the quarry, so that neither hammer nor axe nor any tool of iron was heard in the house while it was being built.

The entrance for the lowest story was on the south side of the house, and one went up by stairs to the middle story, and from the middle story to the third. So he built the house and finished it, and he made the ceiling of the house of beams and planks of cedar. He built the structure against the whole house, five cubits high, and it was joined to the house with timbers of cedar.

Now the word of the LORD came to Solomon, "Concerning this house that you are building, if you will walk in my statutes and obey my rules and keep all my commandments and walk in them, then I will establish my word with you, which I spoke to David your father. And I will dwell among the children of Israel and will not forsake my people Israel." So Solomon built the house and finished it.

He lined the walls of the house on the inside with boards of cedar. From the floor of the house to the walls of the ceiling, he covered them on the inside with wood, and he covered the floor of the house with boards of cypress. He built twenty cubits of the rear of the house with boards of cedar from the floor to the walls, and he built this within as an inner sanctuary, as the Most Holy Place. The house, that is, the nave in front of the inner sanctuary, was forty cubits long. The cedar within the house was carved in the form of gourds and open flowers. All was cedar; no stone was seen. The inner sanctuary he prepared in the innermost part of the house, to set there the ark of the covenant of the LORD. The inner sanctuary was twenty cubits long, twenty cubits wide, and twenty cubits high, and he overlaid it with pure gold. He also overlaid an altar of cedar.

And Solomon overlaid the inside of the house with pure gold, and he drew chains of gold across, in front of the inner sanctuary, and overlaid it with gold. And he overlaid the whole house with gold, until all the house was finished. Also the whole altar that belonged to the inner sanctuary he overlaid with gold.

In the inner sanctuary he made two cherubim of olivewood, each ten cubits high. Five cubits was the length of one wing of the cherub, and five cubits the length of the other wing of the cherub; it was ten cubits from the tip of one wing to the tip of the other. The other cherub also measured ten cubits; both cherubim had the same measure and the same form. The height of one cherub was ten cubits, and so was that of the other cherub. He put the cherubim in the innermost part of the house. And the wings of the cherubim were spread out so that a wing of one touched the one wall, and a wing of the other cherub touched the other wall; their other wings touched each other in the middle of the house. And he overlaid the cherubim with gold.

Around all the walls of the house he carved engraved figures of cherubim and palm trees and open flowers, in the inner and outer rooms. The floor of the house he overlaid with gold in the inner and outer rooms. For the entrance to the inner sanctuary he made doors of olivewood; the lintel and the doorposts were five-sided. He covered the two doors of olivewood with carvings of cherubim, palm trees, and open flowers. He overlaid them with gold and spread gold on the cherubim and on the palm trees.

So also he made for the entrance to the nave doorposts of olivewood, in the form of a square, and two doors of cypress wood. The two leaves of the one door were folding, and the two leaves of the other door were folding. On them he carved cherubim and palm trees and open flowers, and he overlaid them with gold evenly applied on the carved work. He built the inner court with three courses of cut stone and one course of cedar beams.

In the fourth year the foundation of the house of the LORD was laid, in the month of Ziv. And in the eleventh year, in the month of Bul, which is the eighth month, the house was finished in all its parts, and according to all its specifications. He was seven years in building it.

Solomon said that he wanted King Hiram to bring to him "**great stones, costly stones, stones that were hewn to size**" for the building. The Temple was built of stones that were described as "*made ready*" or **prepared** by the stonesquarers. They had to be shaped at the quarry so there would be "*no sound*" made when were put into place in the Temple.

As we saw in Lesson 1, we are the "**stones**". The Holy Spirit uses the Fivefold Ministry in the Church as "**stonesquarers**" to prepare us.

The Fivefold Ministry consists of:

- Apostles
- Prophets
- Teachers
- Pastors
- Evangelists

These gifted ministers are supposed to take the Word of God and in very practical ways show us how to apply The Word to our circumstances. In Ephesians 4:11 the Apostle Paul tells us that the Fivefold Ministers "**equip the Church members**" to do the "**work of the ministry**".

Simply put, this means that the Fivefold Ministers are supposed to prepare us, the "Living Stone" in two ways:

1. Through their teaching

2. Through the example of how they live the Christian Life and to demonstrate it in our daily life.

I believe that the following should be a part of the Vision of every Local Church:

Our Vision is to transform each member into a true Disciple of Jesus and to demonstrate the Kingdom of God in action.

Chapter 4

CIRCUMSTANCES

A second way that The Holy Spirit has chosen to enable us to be transformed from "Reeds" to "Prepared Stones" is by ***allowing us to go through circumstances that are not pleasant.***

We often find ourselves in situations that truly test "what we are made of", i.e. troubles, trials, tribulations, etc. If we have Fivefold Ministers in our lives that are living what we are talking about we have true examples to follow in this process of Transformation.

Also, when we take what we have learned and then apply those teachings to our life situations we see "The Word becoming flesh".

This is what the Apostle Paul was talking about when he wrote

Philippians 2:12 – 13:

> "Therefore, my beloved, as you have always obeyed, not as in my presence only, but now much more in my absence, **work out your own salvation with fear and trembling**; for it is God who works in you both to will and to do for His good pleasure."

In our Transformation Journey we learn why Paul said in

1 Thessalonians 5:16 - 24

"Rejoice always, pray without ceasing, in everything give thanks; for this is the will of God in Christ Jesus for you. Do not quench the Spirit. Do not despise prophecies. Test all things; hold fast what is good. Abstain from every form of evil. Now may the God of peace Himself sanctify you completely; and may your whole spirit, soul, and body be preserved blameless at the coming of our Lord Jesus Christ. He who calls you *is* faithful, who also will do it."

When we first encounter trials and tribulations we usually make a lot of noise. But, as our "Reed Nature" is worked out of us we stop doing that because we realize that it is "God who is at work in us" through those situations.

CAUTION: If you do not learn this most important lesson while you are a Reed you can never become one of the Living Stones that the Lord will use in His Temple because in His House there is to be no complaining!

It is while we are in "the pit" that our Reed Nature is readily revealed. So the "Stonesquarers" begin to work on us and the others who are there. If we are compliant we start the transformation process from "Reeds" to "Stones" but if we don't allow the change to start to take place we are "put on the back burner". This is where many saints backslide… they thing that The Lord doesn't care about them but actually He is very interested in their changing from "Reeds" to "Stones".

The only way to become part of "The Temple of God" the "Reed Nature" has to be worked out of us.

This is a vital truth… In His Church there is to be no murmuring or complaining by His people! We are becoming "Stones" that He can build with rather than "Reeds" that bruise so easily that He cannot use them.

Because He went through all things like we do Jesus went through His testings too…

In **1 Peter 2:6** you will see that the Apostle quotes **Isaiah 28:16** saying that Jesus was a **"tried stone"**. Peter knew what he was talking about! He saw all of Jesus' trials. He was there when Jesus went through those things that brought him to "perfection" (completion).

Peter and the all of the Apostles went through times of testing:

Peter went through his own trials and when he relates that we are living stones there is an implication that we too must go through trials in order to be made ready for the master's use!

Let's look at the

SEVEN CHARACTERISTICS OF THE "STONE NATURE"

Christians who do not allow themselves to be "shaped" by trials and tribulations never become "Stones". They simply stay "Reeds" and although they may "go to Church" they are not the "living stones" that have been Transformed and Equipped so Jesus can place them into the ministry He designed for them in the Church.

This is another vital truth to learn and understand:

My wife, Giovanna, is always quick to point out the truth that although we are all called to serve the Lord in the Church we can never fully do that unless we *"crucify the flesh"* and *"die to self"*.

Without the process of "Death to Self" this taking place we cannot become part of the "building" we know as "the Church".

Reeds Christians have nothing to pass on to the next Generation except to show them how not to live as a victorious Christian!

They don't allow the Holy Spirit to shape them through their trials. They are always murmuring and complaining and they are never transformed. It's such a pity.

Listen to what Paul says here in **Ephesians 2:20 - 22**

> "…having been built on the foundation of the apostles and prophets, Jesus Christ Himself being the chief cornerstone, [21]in whom the whole building, ***being fitted together***, grows into a holy temple in the Lord, [22]in whom you also are being built together for a dwelling place of God in the Spirit.

Stone People know where they belong and they fit in and function there faithfully. And, when they are faithful in little the Lord gives them an increase!

So, Stone People have the following 7 characteristics:

1. They accept their gifts and calling with humility and are not puffed up

2. They start off in an area of "helps" and are supportive and stable

3. They are content not be in "public ministry"

4. They are not blown around the winds of "new doctrines"

5. They do not chase after the latest Christian Fad

6. They are not discouraged by adversity and they are not moved by controversy

7. They are not looking for a "Title" or a lot of fanfare over what they do

You can count on "Stone People" and that's why

Jesus builds with them

Chapter 5

THE STONESQUARER

JUST HOW ARE WE TRANSFORMED?

Since we all start off our Christian life as a "Reed" it's important for us to understand how we are transformed. It is not our reed nature that stops us from growing in God but the way we handle our circumstances that allows God to transform us into "Stone People". We must learn not to resist the Holy Spirit as He works in our lives. This is a twofold work. Let's see this in the Bible:

1. **Ephesians 4:22** He helps us to change our personality (our attitude, the 'spirit' of our mind)

2. **Galatians 5:22-24** He develops our Christ-like character (the fruit of the Spirit)

To see this more clearly let's look at someone who didn't start out too well but became someone great in the Kingdom of God. His name was **Jacob**...

Jacob the Patriarch didn't start out as a stone. The name Jacob literally means "Conniver" or "Schemer". He connived his brother to get the coveted blessing of his father and then he lied to his father to cheat his brother out of his birthright.

There is something about Jacob that some don't see… because his mother overly protected him he could not start the transformation process until she was out of his life. Although she thought she was helping him all of his life she was really hindering him! Do you know someone who is that type of situation today?

When Esau found out what Jacob did he threatened to kill him so his mother told him to run away to his Uncle Laban's house. It was there that he began to "reap" what he "sowed". This is where he meets his own personal **"stonesquarer"**; Uncle Laban. Laban made him work for seven years to get his beloved wife and then he switched the bride with her sister and the evening of the marriage! After that he made him work another seven years and during those years he changed his wages ten times! He had met his match! He had no choice but to go through all of these things. Why? Because truly loved Rachel and he knew if he rebelled against his Uncle Laban that he would never have her as his wife.

Read what Paul said in Philippians 3:13 - 14

"…but one thing I do, forgetting those things which are behind and reaching forward to those things which are ahead, *I press toward the goal for the prize*…"

Like most of us, Jacob had enough of his Uncle Laban's ways and he was tempted to quit many times for sure! But, he saw "the prize" and he was willing to "forget all that was behind him to reach the thing that was his "prize"!

Until we are able to go through whatever
obstacles are in our way in order to keep our
eyes on "the prize" we can never be transformed
from "Reeds" into "Stones".

Jacob eventually left his Uncle Laban but he didn't do it because he had quit! No, he left because he has a vision of something greater for his life. He started to go back home and as he did his past caught up with him and finally the Transformation Process begins.

HOW JACOB BECAME A "STONE PERSON"

The first step to becoming a "stone person" is to have had enough as a "reed person" and be willing to go through hardship in order to have a better life.

This is when God can really begin to "prepare and shape" you! I'm sure if you could have talked to Jacob he would have told you how he had learned his lessons and had changed. But, it is on his way home after he hears that "trouble is coming" that he immediately resorts to his "reed nature". He sends everyone ahead of him and is left all alone. When you are going to be changed by the Lord there is a point when He must get you all alone in order to deal with you.

He wrestles with The Angel of The Lord that night. He has resisted God all his life but now, face to face with this Angel he realizes who he truly is and realizes that, although he is older, he has never changed.

The Angel asks Jacob what his name is he when he replies "Jacob", all of the negative meanings of his name come into his mind. He sees himself as a deceiver, a conniver, a cheat! He faces up to the fact that he is a liar and becomes fed up with himself! He thought he was different but in reality, he is not. He is still the same. He has come to the place where he discovers that he has never changed and he also realizes that he cannot change himself by himself. The truth is that we need the Holy Spirit to help us change.

It was only when the truth was emblazoned into his mind that the angel touched his thigh and Jacob was crippled and it was at that moment that the angel told Jacob that his was no longer "Jacob the

Deceiver". A true change had begun. He was truly being Transformed. He is now Israel, a Prince of God!

All of his desire could not do what facing the truth and relying on The Holy Spirit was able to do. Change had come not by his own efforts but in spite of them. He had finally submitted himself to God enough to have the great inner work of transformation from being a "Reed Person" into becoming a "Stone Person" truly begin!

THE RESULTS OF SUBMITTING TO THE HOLY SPIRIT

Israel always *walked with a limp* after that night to remind him that he once was "Jacob the deceiver" a "Reed Person". As the Holy Spirit changes us there will be a spot in our lives that He will touch and we will always have something to remember our former self with too. It will be a limp of some sort and it will help us to be always remember to be humble and not to "think of ourselves more highly than we ought".

He **received forgiveness** from both his brother and his father. We receive forgiveness for our sins by Jesus our Brother and from God our Father because we broke his heart.

He had the pain and **bitter memory** of never seeing his mother again because she died while he was away. In our lives there are always some things that we cannot regain. These things are the **consequences** of "missing the boat".

He **entered the "Promised Land"**!   He began to live out **Jeremiah 29:11**

> "For I know the plans I have for you, says the LORD, plans for welfare and not for evil, to give you **a future and a hope**".

Once our change starts we see the truth of 2 Corinthians 5:17 The old is passing away and everything is becoming new.

Here are some other Scriptures that come to life as we are being changed...

Deuteronomy 32:9,13

"For the LORD'S portion is his people; Jacob is the lot of his inheritance. He made him ride on the high places of the earth, that he might eat the increase of the fields; and he made him to **suck honey out of the rock, and oil out of the flinty rock**" **Honey** was the sweetest thing in the Bible and speaks of **Character**. **Oil** was necessary for life and it speaks of **the Anointing of God**. Once we begin that transformation we are anointed too. Our character is now being shaped by God through the "stonesquarers".

Ezekiel 16:13

"Thus wast thou decked with gold and silver; and thy raiment was of fine linen, and silk, and broidered work; thou didst eat fine flour, and **honey**, and **oil**: and thou wast exceeding **beautiful**, and thou didst **prosper** into a kingdom." We too begin to prosper in the ways of The Lord no longer seeking the things that the world does… We are seeking "The Kingdom first!

1 Samuel 17:40-49

To kill Goliath David used a smooth stone. A stone that was prepared through tumbling over and over again in the brook. We can **defeat** even **our greatest enemies** when we are "prepared".

Isaiah 32:2

We become like the "shadow of a great rock in a weary land". We become **a comfort to others** who are going through trials as we show them the way to change.

Remember, it is your reed nature that limits your use in God's

Kingdom. So ask the Lord to show you the true meaning of **Romans 8:28**

"And we know that God causes everything to work together for the good of those who love God and are the called out ones who are living out His purposes in their lives."

As we allow God to use the circumstances of our lives to work the change in us we start the transformation from being a "Reed" into a "Stone".

No one put it better than Paul when he used this example:

2 Timothy 2:21

"If a man therefore purge himself from these (the works of the flesh), he shall be a vessel unto honor, sanctified, and meet for the master's use, *someone who has been prepared* for every good work."

This is why the Lord uses "Stone People" to build His Church!

Chapter 6

PILLAR PEOPLE

Chronicles 3:15-17 "also he made before the house two pillars of thirty and five cubits high... And he reared up the pillars before the temple, one on the right hand, and the other on the left; and called the name of that on the right hand **Jachin**, and the name of that on the left **Boaz**."

A pillar is a **support** and it **relieves pressure**. Two is the number of **witness**. God had Solomon rear up two witnesses of His Glory in the front of the House of God. One was called **Jachin** which means "**God Establishes**" and the other was named **Boaz** which means "**Living Strength**".

<u>Jachin</u>**: Established…something that is ordained or appointed permanently**. The Hebrew word brings in the meaning of something that is standing upright.

<u>Boaz</u>**: Living Strength… durability**

A "pillar person" is a person who is appointed by God who stands up as a "strong and enduring, living witness of Christ".

When we look at "Pillar People" through these "types" we will see several key things…

"PILLAR PEOPLE" are

1. Strong
2. Loyal
3. Supportive
4. Faithful
5. A Comfort to others
6. Planted in the Church
7. Established in the "ways" of God

So, How do we become Pillars? We only have to go to the life of the Apostle Peter:

Jesus told Simon the "Reed" that he would no longer be call Simon but Peter "a Stone".

Even after that Peter was often referred to as "Simon Peter"… Why? Because he had not gone through the process of Transformation completely yet!

We can see the truth of **Romans 4:16 – 17** here:

"Therefore it is of faith that it might be according to grace, so that the promise might be sure to all the seed, not only to those who are of the law, but also to those who are of the faith of Abraham, who is the father of us all [17](as it is written, "I have made you a father of many nations") in the presence of Him whom he believed—God, who gives life to the dead *and calls those things which do not exist as though they did*;

We see Peter's Transformation completed in Galatians 2:9

"In fact, **James, Peter, and John, who were known as pillars of the church**, recognized the gift God had given me, and they accepted Barnabas and me as their co-workers."

Genesis 28:10-22   Jacob sets up the Stone he used for his pillow and makes it a **Pillar** and pours oil on it. **A Pillar is a stone stood upright and anointed to be a witness**. We must be standing up in the place where God wants us to be in order to be anointed as a pillar in His House.

We become Pillars by becoming Mature and it takes 5 things for this to happen.

1. **Pillars are People of Praise!**

   Psalm 8:2   "Out of the mouths of babes and sucklings thou hast **established strength**.

Matthew 21:16 "Out of the mouth of babes and sucklings thou hast **perfected praise**".

Jesus equates Praise with Strength!

Maybe this truth will help you understand this Scripture a bit more...

Nehemiah 8:10 "**...the joy of the Lord is your strength**"

Exodus 17:8-12   To win a battle Moses had to keep his hands lifted up (a symbol of praise). His arms got tired and when he let them down the enemy started to win the battle. This shows us that we win our spiritual battles by praising the Lord.

2. **Pillar People are Obedient**
   Psalms 38:10 - 18 Sin (disobedience) robs strength

   My heart beats wildly, my strength fails, and I am going blind. [11]My loved ones and friends stay away, fearing my disease. Even my own family stands at a distance. [12]Meanwhile, my enemies lay traps to kill me. Those who wish me harm make plans to ruin me. All day long they plan their treachery. [13]But I am deaf to all their threats. I am silent before them as one who cannot speak. [14]I choose to hear nothing, and I make no reply. [15]For I am waiting for you, O LORD. You must answer for me, O Lord my God. [16]I prayed, "Don't let my enemies gloat over me or rejoice at my downfall." [17]I am on the verge of collapse, facing constant pain. [18]**But I confess my sins; I am deeply sorry for what I have done.**

Job 17:9   Clean hands (obedience) brings strength

The righteous keep moving forward, and **those with clean hands become stronger and stronger.**

Acts 16:4-5   Obedience establishes us

Then they went from town to town, instructing the believers to follow the decisions made by the apostles and elders in Jerusalem. [5]**So the churches were strengthened in their faith** and grew larger every day.

In Genesis 28

Jacob makes a vow unto God and sets up a pillar as a witness

In Genesis 35:9-15

Jacob goes back in obedience and fulfills his vow. That's when God changed his name to Israel, a Prince of God. He made his vow and kept it. He was obedient.

3. **Pillar People Pray and Persevere**

   Ephesians 6:18   We are told to put on "the whole armor of God" and to pray and persevere.

   2 Corinthians 12:7-9 Paul prayed for deliverance but God told him: "My Grace is sufficient for you" So Paul said that he would "therefore glory in trials" and perseveres!

4. **Pillar People are supportive**

   Exodus 17:8-12   Aaron and Hur rolled a **stone** under Moses and then stood at his side lifting his hands up and **supporting** him. As they did this the battle that was being fought was won. Moses sat on a stone and had two pillars at his side supporting him. Aaron and Hur **relieved the pressure** from Moses and supported him.

   Pillar people are the ones in the Church who are always there.

They are continually helping to establish the Church. Their presence brings strength and joy to everyone around them. They are loyal and you can count of them to be there when you need them. They are upright. They don't cause problems. They help solve them. They are obedient to the Word of the Lord that the Elders bring. They persevere in trials and tribulation and are joyful in them.

5. Pillar People are Overcomers

Revelation 3:12 "Him that **overcometh** will I make a pillar in the Temple of my God"

John 16:33 Jesus said: "In my world ye shall have tribulation: but be of good cheer (joy), I have **overcome** the world."

One area that Pillar people overcome in is their "**emotional tone**". Our emotional tone is a part of our personalities. What this means is that *Pillar People choose* the way they will appear to others.

Pillar People choose to be happy, kind, thoughtful, considerate, patient

They choose not to be impatient, rude, thoughtless, inconsiderate and sad like victims

People who still have a great deal of Reed Nature cannot make these choices. They live as victims of circumstance.

Stone People have a hard time with these choices at times.

But Pillar People overcome their circumstances and themselves.

Chapter 7

OVERCOMERS

There is one thing for sure... Pillar People are the Overcomers that we see in the Bible!

Let me give you an example to make this point clear...

If someone goes to a restaurant and is served by a waiter/waitress who is sullen, not attentive, rude and thoughtless, they will probably get quite upset. Most of us would agree that they have a right to be so. Now, let's say that the person speaks to the manager or owner about the server but is told that the waitress is having a bad day. Does that make it all right? Not really!

What if the manager said; "Well, my employees are not phonies and she is having a bad day and she is not going to act like a phony just to make you happy! This is the way she is and you will just have to accept it." How would that customer react? Not too well, that's for sure!

Now, the customer might say that they don't really care about that. They'll say that she should not bring her poor attitude to work. She is supposed to be a professional and should act like one. And, they may even add that if that server does not choose to leave their problems behind them, they should find a different line of work! Don't you agree?

But now what if the manager said; "Well, she can't help it. When she has a bad day we all just have to put up with it so you will have to put up with it too."

I think that customer is going to find a new restaurant!

This is why Pillar People are Overcomers!

Pillar People know that they are "Ambassadors for Christ" and His Kingdom! There is no other "kingdom" to go to except the devils and we are supposed to rescue people from his kingdom!

Jesus said that he came to **"serve"** and that we are to **"learn of Him."** *He didn't let a "bad day" make him act differently. He chose to act the way he did.* Pillar People are his "servants" and they chose to do the same. They do not bring that kind of junk "to work" with them either.

A "pillar person" is a person who is appointed by God who stands up as a "strong and enduring, living witness of Christ".

So, wherever you are at in your Spiritual Growth, you can set your sights on being a Pillar by allowing The Lord to continue His Work in you!

ABOUT THE AUTHOR

Frank Duprée was raised in Long Island, NY and was Saved in 1969. In 1979, after being in Ministry for several years, he came to New Jersey to start Living Water Church in North Arlington. He was Commissioned and Consecrated as an Apostle and Bishop by the late Dr. Wade E. Taylor, Founder of Pinecrest Bible Training Center.

In January of 2000 he founded Metro Apostolic Network, a fellowship that brings Fivefold Gift Ministers together with Marketplace Ministers and Mature Intercessors. The Network is based in Metro New Jersey and has Apostolic Centers in Brooklyn, NY and Atlanta, GA as well as in Kenya and Pakistan.

Apostle Duprée is a Charter Member of The International Coalition of Apostolic Leaders and in 2014 when the US Coalition of Apostolic Leaders was formed out of ICAL he was appointed as the Senior Administrator working alongside of his close friend and USCAL Convener; Apostle Joseph Mattera.

Apostle Duprée also serves on several other Apostolic Councils based in the NY/NJ Metro area. He works closely with Apostle Bernard Wilks of Newark, NJ, and is a Member of the Executive Council of Transformation Newark and is a Founding Member of The Newark Area Apostolic Council.

You can find out more about Apostle Duprée by visiting his website: www.FrankDupree.com There you will also find numerous teachings and videos. You can also sign up for his monthly e-Newsletter there.